Borrowed Riches

Also by Julie Thorndyke
and published by Ginninderra Press
Mrs Rickaby's Lullaby
Divertimento

Julie Thorndyke

Borrowed Riches

100 tanka

Acknowledgements
Many of the tanka in this collection have been previously published in journals including *ribbons, red lights, Kokako* and *GUSTS*. Others were published as 'bookmark poems' accompanying *Eucalypt: a tanka journal* issues between 2017 and 2020.

Borrowed Riches: 100 tanka
ISBN 978 1 76109 414 9
Copyright © text Julie Thorndyke 2022
Cover photo: Julie Thorndyke

First published 2022 by
GINNINDERRA PRESS
PO Box 3461 Port Adelaide SA 5015
www.ginninderrapress.com.au

This book is dedicated with deep gratitude to
my long-time tanka companions,
Beverley George, Maria Steyn,
Carole MacRury, Carol Raisfeld,
Carmel Summers, Kirsty Karkow
and Dorothy McLaughlin.

in this world
of farewells and sunsets
his hand
still clasped in mine
whatever the weather

a delicate dance
circles into the future
with our children –
when to step forward
when to step back

filaments
of tissue pull apart
and separate…
the long unwrapping
of disintegrating lives

finches feed
in the red coral tree
beside the river
a deep sense of calm
comes with the setting sun

we two –
for as long as water
tumbles down
these rocks
and gravity prevails

leaf canopy
since you left
nothing else
stands between me
and heaven

at sunset
flying foxes circle
and settle…
glowing branches offer
a gum-blossom supper

there's gold
still hanging from the maple
in early July –
late sun through slatted
windows laced with hope

scattered
over this messy desk…
a light trail
of biscuit crumbs
leads me back to my plot

I remember
when even her teapot
was wrapped
in cosy knitted love…
gone now, those skilled hands

once again
we turn to gentle words
for safe harbour…
when even they have faded,
feel the breeze kiss the ocean

pigeons splash
in the wishing well
this grey morning
the ripped lining
of my empty coin purse

the bus rattles
like an old manual
typewriter
tapping out the lines
of commuters' lives

waterfall chimes
sound on my iphone
day and night
poems drip in
for issue twenty-nine

fingertips
drenched in honey
silk turns sticky
causes me to linger
in this autumn sun

soot-black silk
scarlet linen, charcoal tweed
piece by piece
this scrap-bag quilt
yields a story of flame and ash

love rises…
a cloud of purple splendour
in the heat of the day
jacaranda petals
surrender back to the earth

father time
my gentle wrinkled friend
offers patience…
the glad abundance
of our fragrant harvest

leaf-dappled
with light and shade
grateful hands
carry borrowed riches
dream-echoes and life-songs

gardenias
and scented geraniums
poolside
I loiter with skinks
this warm autumn morning

my feet travel
a well-marked path –
the forest
is alive with bright
notes of encouragement

wooden pins
crashing down, bowled
on the alley –
too many young ones
lost on the journey

fast and sleek
this driverless train
in the dark tunnel
wanting to believe
my life is divinely guided

tightly arranged
pictures and photographs
on every wall
a colourful crowd
of faces and memories

first coffee
with a new acquaintance
her wish list
so like mine…
but with many more ticks

his long fingers
weave sounds to soothe
our burned land
this silver-haired minstrel
singing love songs to the earth

no matter
on which cliff I stand
salt winds
tell me we are all
part of one ocean

a wind-up toy
of cheap, pressed tin
gears disengaged –
I wait in stasis
for the switch to be flicked

last kid
chosen for the team
on the fringe
still hoping for
somewhere to belong

fallen leaves
crunch beneath our feet
unnumbered
the years and lives
before colonisation

a single ripple
travels the silent lake
no audience
on that distant shore
to receive nature's music

roads drilled
through Sydney sandstone
this western suburbs girl
always needed
a diamond-tough heart

how am I now
to navigate my life?
one of the stars
by which I steer
has fallen

she lived
a haiku rhythm
in tanka
we glimpsed
her singing heart

rendezvous
beneath the library clock
allotted spans
and shared passion for poems
overlap in this brief gift of time

I drop more pigment
onto my wetted paper
the slow bloom
of indigo-leaved trees
in this wild, mystic forest

crumbs scattered
all through my scribble book
could they hold
a vanilla-scented trail
back to lost childhood

chalk dust
flying from her blackboard
forms a halo
above my teacher's red curls…
new words settle in young minds

the slow ripple
of wave to shore –
a spring afternoon
where winds whip up
all kinds of ambition

high-pitched howl
of the 747
gone again
your sister's sadness
a freshened wound

they rise again
these self-sown bulbs –
in the softness
of dark sandy soil, green
shoots, this easter morning

linchpin
of our family
when you withdrew –
loose wheels rolled down
scattered tracks and byways

from baby babble
emerge three small words
ma, da, ta
building blocks
for a life of thankfulness

so many small
white-cotton kisses
on bright gingham
my grandma's
unconditional love

sand crabs
cluster against the tide
reunited
sisters and brother reprise
childhood's gentle banter

the sweet call
of a butcherbird
each morning
this troublesome
paradox that is you

red camellias –
thirty years on, knowing
which plants
thrive in the clay
this side of our hill

stone tubs
once held the weekly wash
now cradle spring bulbs
each day I find
a new skill to master

maidenhair
fern fronds lying
on the gravel path
…the bouquet I carried
to our wedding vows

an open gate
over stone flags
in the wind
the gardener's ghost
offers a warm welcome

the mild hum
of tyres on tarmac
our last days
of being
and doing together

clinging to
this scarred tree trunk
a bromeliad –
my life wired
just as tightly to yours

dry banksia cone
beside new-season flowers
our son's romance
blooming in the shade
of our long marriage

oat porridge
with chopped pear
the warmth
of autumn love
has so many forms

an unseen owl
hoots through the trees
around the fire
beneath glowing stars
we wait again for the moon

a rusty shovel
parting the weeds
the heft
of your unprompted
words of love

second-hand stall
nothing I want
to purchase
…nothing
I want to give away

a dense blanket
of serrated banksia leaves
underfoot
so many jagged years
you've been my place of comfort

days rush past…
my fingers search for a switch,
button or lever –
any tool to halt
this teeming flow of time

not Manet's
girl at the bar…
my reflection
absorbed in private follies
sips peppermint tea

life's journey
over soft meadows,
jolting rocks…
so blessed to travel this part
of the twisty road with you

never invited,
always insistent –
memories
and this unbidden
breeze troubling my hair

a slink of silk
a flicker of flame
dark windows
guard our secrets
on the orient express

I travel
with no schedule
no map
beyond each new signpost
an unwritten day

even now,
as she tells me
it is her time –
the steady dry warmth
of her hand clasping mine

sometimes sunlight
reaches the cold earth between
the dampest, darkest
cobblestones…
be patient, my weeping heart

no miracles
for her aged body
a slice of mango
a posy of spring flowers,
visit after visit I show up

this sandy path
textured by yesterday's rain
a wagtail
dances in a stand
of flannel flower stems

this impromptu
walking stick of swamp
mahogany –
warm to my touch,
smooth on my mind

pied currawongs
pick over the ashes
of last night's campfire
your questions, my answers
echo round the bloodwoods

this dense silence –
a rough weave
of low velvet tones
just outside
the range of my audition

baby hands
guided in the playground
these seedlings
gently helped
to find the climbing frame

radio news
turned off just as it starts
angled shutters
on my west windows
deflect the rising heat

red ochre dreams
of rocks and shifting sands
carrot soup
on my lunch tray
a bowl of vivid orange

in the treetops
gumnut babies croon
sleepy songs
their mothers' mothers'
mothers knew

all at once
the freesias are finished
just a memory
those heady days
of laughter and friendship

these last months
without wearing her glasses –
more like the child
she once was
than the mother I knew

my new, large handbag –
so similar
in shape and size
to her ever handy
shopping basket

pale blue and white
each smaller than a child's thumb
three china cats
slipped into my pocket
saved from the op shop pile

pale leaves
dripping with light
the gentleness
of our first touch,
your fingers on my cheek

this swirl
of ocean blue –
in the midst
of our turbulence
the red flag of desire

in groups
of two or three –
a congregation
of gum leaves
ready to sing an anthem

citrus peel
thrown on the open fire
sweet freedom
requires us to cast
yesterday into the flame

her white cane
tapping the pavement,
dry umbrella furled,
the blind girl's delighted face
upturned to the wind and rain

I lost the key
to my wind-up train
my father
forged a new one
to keep my world turning

any song
with a backbeat
steadies my heart –
you refill my glass
with red wine

dry heat
after sultry days
yet storm clouds
build, darken,
blow north

a full week
of thunderstorms
each afternoon
growling with electricity
…amid the chaos, your arms

this ivory hook
my grandmother held
in anxious fingers –
I use the same rhythm
to crochet away my fears

straight edges
curved and wavy lines
these odd pieces
just won't coalesce
to solve the puzzle of me

let me lodge
in that hollow place behind
your toughened bark –
rest against that green
and still living wood

the stillness of water
in the early morning –
only in silence
we hear the unsaid
wishes of the heart

we played peekaboo
underneath the old oak tree
tripping on acorns…
my first born
becomes a father

a choice of puddles
in which to stomp –
who knew
middle age held
such possibilities?

I recall old
dance steps, improvise
new moves –
a crescendo of melody
warms my toes

each tarnished spoon
each hand-stitched cloth
tell of days past –
part of your life
always in mine

the stillness
of this evening lake
we remember
what it is
to stop, listen, wait

have you not learned
tomorrow comes, regardless?
lie with me, my love
and dream
on this shared pillow

more fragrant
than spring flowers, the scent
of my lover's arms –
lingering this morning
in a mist of autumn dreams

for a moment,
a snatch of song I almost
remember…
somewhere, in my memory,
also the press of your skin

Julie Thorndyke writes poetry and fiction for children and adults. Editor of *Eucalypt: a tanka journal* since 2017, Julie's books include *Mrs Rickaby's Lullaby* (adult novel), *Divertimento* (short stories) and children's picture books *Waiting for the Night* and *Watching through the Day*.

www.ingramcontent.com/pod-product-compliance
Lightning Source LLC
Chambersburg PA
CBHW050302120526
44590CB00016B/2450